Garfield

Special Delivery

BY: JIM DAVIS

RR
Ravette London

This edition first published by
Ravette Limited 1986

Printed and bound in Great Britain
for Ravette Limited,
3 Glenside Estate, Star Road, Partridge Green,
Horsham, Sussex RH13 8RA
by William Clowes Limited, Beccles and London.

ISBN 0 948456 31 0

Special Delivery

In the next 80 pages of canned laughter you'll see Garfield receive his 'just desserts' when he dishes out a huge helping of his own brand of good humour. You'll pack up with laughter with his funniest deliveries!

© 1980 United Feature Syndicate, Inc.

I'M GOING OUT, GARFIELD. THE WOMEN WILL BE HYSTERICAL OVER ME

THAT OUTFIT'S HYSTERICAL

WHAT DO YOU THINK OF MY ATTIRE?

IT COULD USE SOME ALTERATION

LET'S TUCK THAT TIE IN AND ADD SOME VENTS TO THE SLEEVES

3·29

© 1981 United Feature Syndicate, Inc

A SMART CAT KNOWS JUST HOW FAR TO GO WITHOUT CROSSING OVER THE LINE

PERHAPS A MORE RAKISH TILT TO THE HAT

JIM DAVIS

UH OH. I'LL NEVER MAKE IT ACROSS THAT SUNBEAM AWAKE

NOTHING VENTURED, NOTHING GAINED

4-5

© 1981 United Feature Syndicate.

Z

POOMP!

COME ON, GARFIELD LET'S GO FOR A WALK

Z

Z   Z

JIM DAVIS

HELLO THERE, NERMAL

GARFIELD! WHERE'S NERMAL? YOU DIDN'T STUFF HIM IN THAT BREADBOX DID YOU?

JIM DAVIS

1-10

THANK HEAVENS!

WHAT KIND OF AN ANIMAL DOES JON THINK I AM?

© 1982 United Feature Syndicate, Inc.

URF

OH, SHUT UP, ODIE

HERE I AM IN THE LAND OF LARGE BREAKFASTS

THIS GIANT PANCAKE SURE TASTES GOOD

WHAT A NICE DREAM

JIM DAVIS   1-24

WHERE'S MY BLANKET?

POOKY, WITH YOUR HELP WE SHOULD GET JON'S STEAK DINNER TONIGHT

DON'T WORRY, OLD BUDDY, I'LL SEW YOU BACK UP WHEN WE'RE DONE

JIM DAVIS

2-7

TAP TAP

© 1982 United Feature Syndicate, Inc.

LET ME GET THIS STRAIGHT... YOU SAY YOUR CAT'S TEDDY BEAR ATE YOUR DINNER?

BIGGEST APPETITE FOR A TEDDY BEAR I'VE EVER SEEN

YOU KNOW, YOU'RE A VERY LUCKY CAT, GARFIELD

YOU HAVE JUST ABOUT EVERYTHING A CAT COULD WANT

YOU HAVE YOUR SANCTUM SANCTORUM

MY HIDEY-HOLE

YOU HAVE YOUR TEDDY BEAR

MY CONFIDANT

YOU HAVE YOUR DOG

MY SCRATCHING POST

JIM DAVIS   2-14

AND YOU HAVE ME, YOUR LOVING COMPANION

MY FOOD-FIXER AND LITTER BOX CHANGER

PHOBIAS ARE FUNNY THINGS

I AM ABSOLUTELY FEARLESS EXCEPT WHERE SPIDERS ARE CONCERNED

HELLO, SNAKE

HOW ARE YOU?

ISN'T THAT STRANGE? SPIDERS SCARE ME, BUT SNAKES DON'T SCARE ME

2-28

JIM DAVIS

NOW SNAKES SCARE ME

WHAT DO YOU THINK, GARFIELD?

DON'T ASK

THERE'S NOTHING LIKE CAMPING OUT IN COLD WEATHER

THAT'S FOR SURE

JIM DAVIS

3-7

AS THE TEMPERATURE DROPS, THE CIRCULATION GETS GOING

AND THE FEET GET NUMB

© 1982 United Feature Syndicate, Inc

THIS IS NATURE AT HER BEST!

I'D SETTLE FOR LESS

WE HAVE EVERYTHING... OUR FIRE, OUR SHELTER...

OUR COFFEE ON A STICK

CHOMP!
SLURP! GULP!

Z

STAY OUT OF
MY DREAMS

© 1982 United Feature Syndicate, Inc.

JIM DAVIS

3-28

© 1982 United Feature Syndicate, Inc.

4-4

© 1982 United Feature Syndicate, Inc.

SNAP!

BLAT!

5-30

JIM DAVIS

IS IT WINDY OUT, GARFIELD?

NOT SO YOU'D NOTICE

GARFIELD

I LOVE YOU, BUNNY RABBIT

I LOVE YOU, TOO, DEER

I LOVE YOU ALL

JIM DAVIS 6-6

© 1982 United Feature Syndicate, Inc.

WHAT THE...?

I BROUGHT SOME FRIENDS HOME FOR DINNER

YAWN

DID YOU EVER HAVE A TIME WHEN YOU WISH YOUR PETS COULD SPEAK?

© 1982 United Feature Syndicate, Inc.

JIM DAVIS 6-20

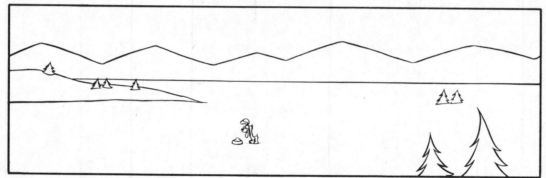

© 1982 United Feature Syndicate, Inc.

JIM DAVIS

7-11

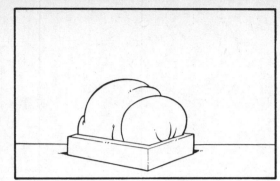

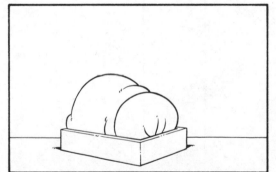

GARFIELD

IT'S SHOW TIME!

SOME DAY I'M GONNA BE THE GREATEST CATERWAULER IN THE WORLD. THEY'RE GONNA CALL ME "CATS WAULER"

ROWR!

CHUKONG!

AROOO

WHOCK!

WHY DO YOU DO IT, GARFIELD?

DUES. I'M JUST PAYING MY DUES

JIM DAVIS 8-15 © 1982 United Feature Syndicate, Inc.

© 1982 United Feature Syndicate, Inc.

JIM DAVIS 9-26

GARFIELD®

WHAT'S THIS?

HERE'S AN INTERESTING ARTICLE ABOUT THE ANCIENT PRACTICE OF CANNIBALISM

LOVELY

CAN YOU IMAGINE WHAT LIFE WAS LIKE THEN?

TRAVELING SALESMEN WERE CALLED "MEALS ON WHEELS"

HAVING THE BOSS OVER FOR DINNER HAD AN ENTIRELY DIFFERENT MEANING

IT SAYS HERE CERTAIN TRIBAL SOCIETIES ALSO ATE CATS

© 1982 United Feature Syndicate, Inc.

JIM DAVIS

I CAN HEAR A DINER COMPLAINING, "OH, WAITER, THERE'S A FLEA COLLAR IN MY SOUP"

THAT'S NOT FUNNY

10-10

IF I DISGUISE MYSELF AS A BIRD, I SHOULD BE ABLE TO GET CLOSE ENOUGH FOR AN EASY LUNCH

GLUK
GLUK
GLUK

SWIM FINS

WADDLE
WADDLE

JIM DAVIS

10-31

© 1982 United Feature Syndicate, Inc.

HOW ABOUT A SHOT OF FLEA POWDER, GARFIELD?

IF YOU CAN HIT A MOVING TARGET

JIM DAVIS

SCREEEE

GARFIELD

11-14

I GUESS IT'S SAFE TO EAT

GARFIELD

GOTCHA!

I GUESS I PULLED A GOOD ONE ON GARFIELD

© 1982 United Feature Syndicate, Inc.

GUESS AGAIN, SUCKER

ALL RIGHT!

I LOVE FLOWERS!

I LOVE TO TIPTOE THROUGH TULIPS

DIVE THROUGH DAISIES

JIM DAVIS 12-5

ROMP THROUGH ROSES

© 1982 United Feature Syndicate, Inc.

YOUR CAT BROKE'M, YOU BOUGHT'EM, BUDDY

Floral Shoppe

PUT SOME PANSIES ON THE TAB, TOO

GOOD MORNING, GARFIELD. I'M SO HAPPY YOU CAN SHARE THIS GLORIOUS MORNING WITH ME

MICHELANGELO WOULD GIVE UP PAINTING IN A MINUTE IF HE SAW THE CANVAS MOTHER NATURE HAS RENDERED JUST FOR US TODAY

CHIRP CHIRP

JUST LISTEN TO THE SYMPHONY OF SOUND FROM NATURE'S FLUTE SECTION

AND THE PERFECT SIGHTS AND SOUNDS ARE PERFUMED WITH THESE LOVELY FLOWERS. WHAT DO YOU THINK, GARFIELD?

JIM DAVIS

12-19

YOU REALLY DON'T CARE, DO YOU?

BINGO

© 1982 United Feature Syndicate, Inc.

GARFIELD, WHERE ARE YOOOOOOU?

GET OUT OF THE BREADBOX, GARFIELD!

GET OUT FROM UNDER THE CHAIR, GARFIELD!

JIM DAVIS

7-22

GARFIELD, YOU KNOW I HATE IT WHEN YOU HIDE FROM ME!

© 1984 United Feature Syndicate, Inc.

OH, WELL, I'LL FIND HIM SOONER OR LATER. THERE'S ONLY SO MANY PLACES A FAT SLOB LIKE HIM CAN HIDE

GET OFF THE BOOKCASE, GARFIELD

© 1984 United Feature Syndicate, Inc.

JIM DAVIS

9-30

© 1984 United Feature Syndicate, Inc.

10-7

JIM DAVIS

HEY, HUBERT! REBA! COME HERE, QUICK!

PLAY COWBOY AND HORSY, BOYS. DO A HANDSTAND, GARFIELD. BALANCE ON GARFIELD, ODIE

SAD

HE SHOULD GET OUT OF THE HOUSE MORE

© 1984 United Feature Syndicate, Inc.

JiM DAViS

11-25